A Spiritual Handbook for the Modern Era

ALSO BY KATE ROUSE

The Diary of a Happy Dropout

Still a Happy Dropout

Mya meets Elin or Love meets Light

A little bit of Poetry

A Spiritual Handbook

for the

Modern Era

Kate Rouse

ZEPHYR
Publications

A SPIRITUAL HANDBOOK FOR THE MODERN ERA
Copyright © KATE ROUSE 2013

First Edition by Zeus Publications, Queensland, Australia, 2013
Second Edition by Zephyr Publications, Queensland, Australia, 2019

The National Library of Australia Cataloguing-in-Publication

Author: Rouse, Kate
Title: A spiritual handbook for the modern era

ISBN: 978-0-6487165-0-1 (pbk)

Subjects: Self-help techniques
Spiritual Life
Self-actualization (Psychology)
Dewey Number: 158.1
All Rights Reserved

No part of this book may be reproduced in any form, by photocopying or by any electronic or mechanical means, including information storage or retrieval systems, without permission from both the copyright owner and the publisher of this book.

This book is a work of non-fiction.
The author asserts her moral rights.

Desktop publishing—Wendy Blake 2019
© Cover design—Wendy Blake 2019

For Shayne, my earthy anchor

And for all who are seeking meaning and purpose within the veneer of everyday life

Acknowledgements

A huge thank you to my life partner, Shayne Hall, for believing in me and supporting my dreams. Thank you to Ray and Anne Pullinger, whose lovely home near the ocean in Queensland provided a haven for the writing of this little book. Thank you to the ocean for giving me peace and clarity and my horses for keeping me grounded and dreaming. Mardi McCarthy provided encouragement with her enthusiasm for the book which I greatly appreciate. Positive words from my wise friend, Gordon Gannon, and my sweet farmer friend, laughing Graham Trewin, helped to keep me focused and believing. Thank you to my aunt, Sal Huxtable, for her interest and support. Thank you to everyone at Zeus Publications for birthing the first edition into the world. A special thank you to Wendy Blake for her desktop publishing assistance and designing the beautiful cover. Thank you to our property, Bahwyn Horse Stud, for giving me space and lucidity to complete the second edition. Finally, I would like to thank my beautiful mother, Alice Rouse, who has always been there for me and supported my goals despite me not following conventional paths.

About the author

The eldest of four sisters, Kate Rouse grew up in Albury and on a small farm at Table Top, New South Wales, Australia. She had a happy childhood with freedom to explore nature and enjoy life with horses that were a huge part of her life then as they still are today.

After completing a BA and Dip Ed at the University of New England, Armidale, Kate worked at Mt Hotham and Mt Buffalo in various roles and travelled extensively throughout the world for 12 years, interspersed with teaching English in Japan and casual teaching in New South Wales and Victoria. She self-published two travelogues in the 1990's.

During the following 12 years Kate worked as a teacher, Aboriginal Education Worker, youth worker, pool manager, factory hand and receptionist. She travelled in Australia with her partner, Shayne, completed Certificate IV in Community Welfare, a Diploma of Counselling and a Fine Arts Certificate.

At Christmas 2010, Kate was struck down with pneumonia and during this time she contemplated her mortality. Slowly recuperating while house-sitting in Queensland, Kate began to think about what she would write in a book if her life was coming to its finality when the idea of, "A Spiritual Handbook for the Modern Era," emerged in 2012. Kate wanted to help others who were experiencing trouble or confusion and provide some clarity with relevance to the sometimes complicated and often demanding era we find ourselves in today. Kate published the book with Zeus Publications in 2013.

Kate and Shayne now live in Queensland where they are establishing a small horse stud. Living with Chronic Fatigue and its many challenges, Kate is still pursuing her dream of being a writer and artist. She has experienced life broadly, felt life deeply and studied spirituality from an early age. Kate and Shayne share their lives with Teuco, a talkative blue parrot, Whispit and Sox, mischievous tabby cats, and 12 beautiful horses.

This is a little book offering insight to living a spiritually aware life cultivating growth of the soul and greater peace and happiness for humanity and our beautiful planet.

GOD

God is in me

Around me

In you

Around you

In everything, around everything

God connects

Creates meaning

My temple is in the desert

My church is on the mountain

My synagogue is by the river bank

My mosque touches the ocean

In Nature I find God

In Stillness, Simplicity

And my love pours forth

Connecting me, feeling I am in God and God is in me

Oneness, available to all humanity—ready to be united

in the love of one God who does not discriminate

Contents

Chapter One
For children and their parents.. 3

Chapter Two
For teenagers.. 17

Chapter Three
Young adults and on a bit 33

Chapter Four
Middle and later life... 61

Chapter Five
The world as it is 71

Chapter Six
Nature 75

Chapter Seven
The spiritual life 81

Chapter Eight
Looking forward... 95

Chapter One
FOR CHILDREN AND THEIR PARENTS

Child

Find your talents and foster them but within realistic limits so that you enjoy them—that it does not become a painful struggle and destroy the outflow of your gift's bounty.

Parents

Foster your child's talents but within her desires, otherwise great potential may be harmed. It is your child's journey, not yours, but you pave the way providing opportunity for talents to flourish.

Creativity connects you to God. You can be creative through writing, artwork, play, sport, cooking, exploring, experimenting, building, music, dance, drama or gardening. Creativity leads to great peace and happiness.

Empathy

Try to think of others. Whatever you say or do to another human has an effect. Put yourself in the position of the other person and imagine how he would feel as a result of your words or actions.

With empathy in mind, and greater awareness, the world would become a more loving and caring place. Have this same regard for all animals and nature—to care for all of God's Earth and her creatures.

Bullying is a growing and terribly destructive problem. With greater empathy this could be minimised. Parents, please encourage your children to think of the results of their words and actions and imagine themselves in the place of others.

To the victim of bullying

The bully's ego is causing destructive behaviour. Remember, you are loved, special and important, a shining star. Remove yourself from the situation and seek help from friends, teachers, parents or school counsellors. Don't suffer alone.

If this happens through the internet or phone let others know and action needs to be taken immediately. Don't let the bully destroy you. You are the strong one. Seek help, surround yourself in love and light will overcome this darkness.

Parents

Maintain vigilance over your child's emotional wellbeing. If you notice a change, talk to him and then maybe his teacher, school counsellor or principal. If bullying is occurring prompt action needs to be taken.

Vigilance is required regarding internet and mobile phone use. Speak with your child and be a part of social networking. Communication and awareness will help greatly in this area.

To the bully

You need to try to feel empathy for your victim. Put yourself in her shoes. Seek help from a counsellor and you too may move forward in your life.

Remember to play

Activity of a physical nature is important for the body, mind and soul. Don't become chained to technology—the internet, television, video games, phones—they are tools, not real life. Remember to explore and play outside. Have fun and God will be smiling.

Health

Eat a healthy diet of vegetables, fruit, grains, meat, fish, nuts, seeds, healthy fats and dairy. Minimise sugar, fast food and unhealthy snacks.

Regular exercise through play, sports or dance is important. Keep your body healthy through good nutrition and exercise and you will have greater energy and a clearer mind. This is all positive for body, mind and soul.

Respect

Children need to learn to respect their siblings, friends, elders, teachers and other people in general. With greater respect there will be greater harmony at home, at school, in society and in the world.

Child abuse

Children need to be made aware of what is unacceptable abnormal behaviour from adults and other children and to tell a trusted adult if it occurs so appropriate action can be taken without delay. They need to be encouraged to seek help despite threats from the abuser.

Wilderness

If possible, it may be beneficial for children to experience wilderness to learn to respect and love nature and carry that feeling into adult life to lead a harmonious existence on this troubled planet. In an untouched rainforest or on a coral reef life feels complete, all-encompassing, as God intended.

Responsibility

As children grow older it is beneficial for them to have responsibilities around the home as this will help prepare them for adult life. The responsibility of caring for a pet is also of value as they learn to look after another creature, develop love for it and hopefully all animals.

When a child loses a pet, this is a good learning ground for the future experience of grief and loss in whatever form it may take. The connection with pets will hopefully foster a love for all of God's creatures and their habitats.

Spirituality

Children can pray, create, meditate and connect to God. Through that connection they can become beings of light illuminating the world.

Chapter Two
FOR TEENAGERS

Sensitivity

By developing empathy, you will cultivate your sensitivity. Be aware and sensitive towards the wellbeing of your friends, other kids, family, teachers and elders. Treat others with dignity and respect as well as animals and the environment. This may enhance the growth of your soul.

Life is a gift as is your body which also requires respect and care. Cigarettes, drugs and alcohol (beyond moderation) harm your body and diminish your soul's progress.

Body Consciousness

The media and fashion industry have created the "ideal" image of the thin athletic body, but this is unnatural. Aim for your *ideal* body weight as advised by your doctor. It is what is on the inside that counts, your shining human spirit. Be healthy through a balanced diet and exercise, but don't let this snowball into bulimia and anorexia—terrible diseases of the modern western world. Skeletal images are shocking—there is no beauty in that. Seek help early if you are heading that way, or help others who may need to do so. It is the real you inside that counts, and you need to try to love yourself and remember, that God loves you and is waiting for your love.

Obesity

Obesity is a huge and growing problem in the world. Lack of exercise and processed foods contribute to this. If you are overweight, see your doctor for advice regarding diet and exercise and she will help you put in place a plan to achieve your *ideal* weight and maintain it. It can be extremely difficult but worth it in the long run as when you feel lighter you will feel more confident and have more energy to pursue your goals and dreams.

Peer pressure

Sometimes others may pressure you to do things you don't want to do, such as smoking. Stand your ground. If they continue to coerce you, you would be better off finding new friends.

Individuality

Difference enriches life whether it be through ethnicity, cultural aspects, sexual preferences, religion, personal preferences of any kind, creativity bringing forth your spirit to the world.

You may be criticised and teased for your individuality, but do not let this hurt you—you are loved by God as you are and you are free to express your individuality in the modern western world. Those who tease or bully lack empathy, true confidence and awareness of themselves as spiritual beings.

Decision making and goal setting

When you have a decision to make it is useful to write down the potential alternative outcomes of the decision and all the negative, neutral and positive impacts. With these in mind the decision will be easier.

Goals are useful, and when you have worked them out—writing them on a card and pinning them up in your room helps to keep you focused.

When goal setting, it can be beneficial to break down the process of reaching the goal into little steps so you progress slowly and steadily towards your desired outcome. Writing these things down is helpful to refer back to and keep on track.

Subject choice

This is important as it sets the beginning of your academic pathway. Choose subjects that resonate with your soul—that interest you, that you are good at, that allow your creative fire to burn. Of course, you can change later but having that awareness in your decision making at subject choice time will be of great benefit now and in the future.

Study

Work as hard as you can at school as there will be benefits later on, but don't let it hamper your happiness and peace of mind. If the burden becomes too much to bear, seek counselling, change subjects, repeat, or maybe alter your goals so they don't push you beyond your limits.

When studying, a good idea is to study for 50 minutes and then take a break for 10 minutes doing something totally different, like a walk outside or tidying your room. You will return fresh and ready to learn some more.

After completing school education

When you have completed your school studies it may be useful to get an apprenticeship, go to TAFE, college or university. It is a competitive world out there and qualifications count. Of course, it is not essential, but it may be beneficial to have that backstop.

Contraception

Learn about the available methods and ensure you are prepared with the method that suits you and your lifestyle. You may think you don't need such things but at times the unplanned event may happen.

Unplanned pregnancy

is a terrible shock and a very emotional time. Ensure you seek help from a sympathetic doctor, a family member if possible, friends or counsellors—anyone you can confide in. Take your time making decisions and make sure you have a peaceful place to let clarity through. Think about the outcomes of your decision and how it will make you feel in one year or ten. Don't be hard on yourself, and remember, God loves you, and will do so, whatever choice you make.

Adoption

There are many great potential parents out there eager to adopt, but that has to be a soul-felt decision as it can leave you broken and your child may feel rootless and confused when he discovers he is adopted. There are many ways to bridge the gap and it may be the best solution for everyone involved. Think carefully, think slowly and think soulfully.

Pregnancy termination

If that feels right for you, seek medical assistance. If it doesn't, be careful not to be pressured by those around you as the result can be a heavy emotional scar, difficult to heal, and grief, difficult to resolve. If you require a termination, seek counselling and your doctor can help organise things, or there is information in the phone book and on the internet.

Post pregnancy termination

Immediately post-termination, hopefully you can be in a safe loving place and nurture yourself as your body and soul readjusts to the changes you have just experienced. Take time, try to be peaceful and release any emotions as they arise. Be gentle with yourself.

If you are experiencing difficult emotions post-termination, seek counselling, attend a Rachel's Vineyard Retreat (www.rachelsvineyard.org.au) and speak with a spiritual worker. These things can help, but it can be a slow hard road to tread, and in the end, there has to be forgiveness. God forgives you and you need to forgive those involved, and greatest of all, yourself. Love yourself and let God's light and love through to break the clouds of darkness shrouding your heart so that it can sing again songs of love to your soul, God and the world.

Rituals may help as in other areas of your life. Use flowers, rocks, ornaments, religious icons, letters, fire, water, soil, whatever feels right. Speak, sing, dance, write your thoughts and feelings and ritual will help cleanse, release and bring you back into wholeness. While broken, you are unable to progress wholeheartedly in your physical or spiritual life.

Depression

From time to time, you may experience black emotion that leaves you feeling isolated, misunderstood and hopeless. Seek help from counsellors, your doctor, friends and family. Don't let it destroy you. There is a light at the end of the darkest tunnel. In your darkest moment you will not agree with that, but really, truly, there is. Don't give up. God is there for you. He will listen too.

Suicidal thoughts

If you have suicidal thoughts of any kind seek help immediately. Things may be terrible, but PLEASE remember the gift that is your life and there is something to live for—your family, friends, pets, your passions.

Spirituality

In your teenage years you may begin seeking the spirit within you and God surrounding all that is. Through joining religious or spiritual groups you may explore this aspect further and rejoice in your faith in God.

Prayer, meditation, reading spiritual books, ritual and communing in nature may all enhance your spiritual life. As you discover the God within you and around you, you will become more composed, peaceful, aware and happy.

Whilst meeting like-minded souls your life will be enriched as your soul's journey is enhanced.

As your spiritual bloom blossoms, God will be smiling.

Chapter Three
YOUNG ADULTS AND ON A BIT

Awareness in decision making

When a decision has to be made, especially those of a pivotal nature, take your time. Rushed decisions don't always lead to ideal outcomes.

If emotions are strongly involved, try to stand back from them and see the situation as clearly as possible.

Write down the alternatives and different impacts. The right choice should arise like a new leaf unfurling, ready to face its new life, unfettered by confusion.

Goal setting

Writing down your goals helps. Keep that card somewhere prominent. The little steps, like the rungs on a ladder, can also be scribed, to help you achieve your life's dreams. Dreams are important. They can sustain you. Do not give up on your dreams.

Balance in life

At this stage you may tend to rush into life at full force, wanting to taste all it has to offer with gusto, but remember balance—through diet, exercise, limiting undesirable substances and nurturing your spiritual life. Balance gives equanimity to your soul, enhancing your spiritual journey.

Cigarettes, drugs and alcohol diminish you and cloud your clarity, cutting you off from a soulful life.

Gambling can also cut you off from a spiritual life and can be very destructive when it becomes an addiction. Poker machines were designed to lure you in and the chance of winning a decent amount of money is close to zilch. Don't be influenced by others to follow this path as it may harm you and those close to you. If you fail and fall down here, seek counselling and hopefully you can overcome this urge.

Work

Ideally, you would be in a job you love, something that comes naturally to you, so everything else falls into place. Otherwise, take steps to change by studying, volunteering or taking a part-time job in the preferred field.

Whatever gifts you have, try to make them of use to help others. Try to do what makes you happy.

Nowness

Being present-centred, so you are totally present to those you are in communication with will be of great benefit to those around you as they feel attended to. Being present-centred to the work you are doing, whatever you are doing, enhances your soul's journey as you are focussed on the *now*.

Nowness can be attained through creativity—being absorbed in painting, writing, baking, conversation—or sport, such as skiing down a mountain, catching a football, snorkelling on a reef or through meditation techniques or communing in nature. Carry that nowness into everyday life and the results can only be positive. When you are washing the dishes or hanging out the washing, remember that nowness.

Materialism

You may be driven at this stage to obtain more and more material objects, but in the end, they can enslave you. You spend so much time caring for these objects they may distract you from your spiritual journey and spending quality time with others.

The richest man on Earth is unlikely to be the happiest. People with great riches often have great problems and fall prey to the darkest side of life—drug and alcohol abuse, gambling and psychological problems. This is so often seen amongst the famous—musicians and actors. They have all the money in the world and fame, which is not necessarily so desirable. They have opportunities abounding, but they are so often victims of their own lifestyles and psychological capacity to cope.

Be wary of desiring fame as it is not always the golden pathway painted by the media.

Simplicity can lead to happiness, things in moderation and time for a soulful life.

Passion

Everyone needs something to be passionate about, to enliven the fire in your soul. If you don't have a passion, seek one out. Nurture it and there will be rewards and happiness.

Travel is a great way to open the mind and learn of the variety of life. Through seeing other ways of being with awareness and sensitivity you will be nourished on a soul level. It will also help with developing empathy. You may learn greater respect and love for nature as displayed by people living close to her, such as the Mongolian nomads or Amazon Indians. These people know how important it is to care for the environment and their lives are entwined within it.

Judgement

As you proceed through life you may judge yourself in terms of your progress—whether it be academic, materially, career success, even spiritually—and you may do so in terms of others' attainments. If you have not reached a certain goal by a certain time you may be self-punishing which may diminish your feelings of self-worth. Don't judge yourself in negative terms—just keep moving steadily forward, at times stopping and taking things in, possibly sliding back a little, but like the tortoise, you will get there in the end, somehow. Possibly your goals may change which alters the canvas of your life.

Life is like a river, meandering this way and that. Sometimes the water may pause at a bend, or in a lake, but eventually it reaches the ocean.

Judging others is a waste of time and energy. They are living a life they have chosen and judgement has no point.

Envy is also of little use. Being at peace with where you are and your destination is the soulful way.

Do the best that you can in the circumstances you find yourself in. Don't punish yourself if you fall short of expectations.

Emotions

This is also a time of life when emotions can often take over. They play a role in your decision making, but be careful not to let them cloud the process.

If depression or anxiety strike, seek counselling and try to remember the God within you and all-encompassing.

If you feel depression is taking over your life, exercise helps, as does having little goals. Try not to be hard on yourself. Being in nature can also be of benefit and trying to do what you love, though you probably don't feel you love it anymore. However, as you slowly undertake your previously-loved pursuit, some inkling of satisfaction and sunniness may begin to re-emerge. Volunteering may also aid recovery. There is light at the end of that dark tunnel—I promise you. If you are on the spiritual path, spiritual work is healing. Nowness helps greatly. Focus on the little things. Try not to become enslaved by the past or concerned for the future. You will get better with little steps. You are loved by God and He wants you to heal as you learn to love yourself, Him and all of his world.

Having awareness of your negative emotions, how they affect you and those around you, and then healing that part of you is soulful work and part of a soulful life. Overcoming your fear, anger, any other negative emotion, will lead to greater harmony and peace on all levels.

Gratitude

Sometimes, when life seems so difficult and you are in a situation that seems not so great for you, having gratitude can be helpful—being grateful for your family, friends, pets, having a roof over your head, food on the table, safety, a beautiful sunset, leading a spiritual life.

Appreciating the little things in your life can be beneficial and healing for your soul.

Illness

Sometimes illness strikes and it may take a long time to recover, sometimes a lifetime. Seek all the medical help you can, try alternative methods and look at your diet and lifestyle. It can be difficult to rest, but that may be your only choice and it may be an opportunity for spiritual growth through reading, prayer and meditation.

Acceptance helps. If you can't change a situation, acceptance leads to peace of mind and a more positive outlook and strength to cope.

Acceptance is important in life in general. Things will not always be as you desire. If you are not happy in a situation, try to accept it. Take steps to change and have patience. Life consists of ups and downs, and to keep on an even keel, useful tools are acceptance, gratitude and patience.

Relationships can be very exciting at this time—exploring life with another human is enriching and can be life and soul enhancing, but discernment is necessary. If you feel drained on any level by a relationship, and after attempts to solve a lack of harmony fail, it may be best to end the relationship.

If the other person is leading you down a destructive path of dark activity, that may be a signal to end the relationship. Seek counselling, try whatever you can, but don't let a relationship diminish you or your light-filled journey towards God.

If you are experiencing abuse on any level, seek help. No one deserves this. Make sure you let others know what is going on and don't stay where you or your children will be harmed.

Sometimes a relationship may sour with weariness, but try to remember what drew you to that person in the first place and relive that admiration. Take out special time together at a restaurant, on a picnic, a walk in the mountains and remember why you love that man or woman beside you and nourish the partnership that you share. Life is a ride of ups and downs and through them you will grow.

Change

Life is about change. It cannot be otherwise. Challenging situations may seem impossible to deal with at times, but they are great opportunities for growth and progress— mentally, emotionally and spiritually. With greater awareness and clarity, you can move forward with optimism.

Animals and the environment

As you respect and care for other human beings, you need to respect and care for animals and the environment we live in.

The Earth needs our care more than ever and requires love and respect, otherwise the future of our planet is not optimistic. Living in harmony and balance is the way forward.

It is so sad that so many animals are endangered and their habitats are being so rapidly destroyed. Time is running out and humanity needs to change its incessant desire for more and more things and processed food. It needs to reduce population growth to turn back the clock to a time when there was greater balance. Sustainability must be the way.

Home is your temple

Wherever you live it is your temple, whether it be a tent, a caravan, an apartment, a house or a cabin. As you keep it clean and ordered there will be space in your mind and heart. Clutter creates confusion and clouds the mind.

From time to time, cleaning out the home—ridding yourself of the unnecessary—is cleansing on all levels, and may involve some release of the past.

As you care for your home, your temple, you care for your soul. Cleaning the home can be loving, a ritual and a meditation. Humans have been dusting, sweeping, mopping and gardening for millennia. As you do these things you may feel connected to the ancient, the simple, the humble—to the continuity of human life. As you put your hands in the soil you may feel connected to the Earth and all that is. Tickle the Earth and make her laugh.

Biological clock and mothering

If you desire children, take care not to leave it until it is too late. The trend in the western world towards late child bearing has left many women childless with feelings of grief and loss for the unborn child and mother they will never be. If this desire is strong within you, you need to be planning by 32 if everything is well with you and your partner on a gynaecological level.

Stay-at-home mums and dads are doing a wonderful job. Bringing up children in a safe, loving and soul-filled way is one of the most important jobs on Earth. When you can, if at all possible, put aside some special time each week just for you, whether it be a dance class, playing sport, coffee with a friend or walking in a forest—something that nourishes your soul.

Childless

If you find yourself childless and you didn't desire this outcome and there is no opportunity for adoption, you may feel grief and loss for your unborn children and the mother and father you will not be. There may be a big hole in your life that you hoped to be filled with nurturing your children and their cries and laughter.

Seek counselling as your boat's anchor has become stuck in some dark sludge that can be difficult to sail out of, but once you do so you may be able to find peace with this situation. You can be grateful for your relationship, other children in your life, peace and quiet for study, prayer, contemplation and meditation, time for pursuit of your own interests or travel—endless possibilities and freedom.

You need to channel your energy in other ways—through work, relationships of all types, charity work, creative pursuits. There are so many opportunities, and this time, your energy needs to be put to good use elsewhere than having children. This is a great opportunity for soulful work and a soulful life.

Miscarriage is a natural process and it is normal to feel grief and loss for your baby. Don't be hard on yourself and take time to nurture yourself and heal. Take it slowly and lovingly and seek counselling if you are overwhelmed.

Singles

You may desire a relationship, or may be happy alone. Either way, your time alone is a time of great freedom as you make choices, plans and pursue dreams. You have a great capacity to cultivate a soulful life and live in harmony with God's love.

If you desire a relationship, it may arise at the most unexpected place and time. Cherish your alone time. It can be very special.

Magic and flow

As you work towards your dreams, and as long as it feels right, you will be amazed at times how life seems to be magical and flow effortlessly. You are living as you should and your energy is working well for you. The right people, opportunities and places will arise as needed and your light will shine.

Spirituality

By now you may be aware of the listener behind the thoughts—the observer of your mind. The stillness beyond is where you can spend time in meditation, through creativity, sports, in the natural world or through nowness in such simple things as watching the water from the hose touch the garden without thoughts intruding. The more practise the better and greater harmony will enter your life on all levels. It will also create greater harmony between humans and a more peaceful world.

Chapter Four
MIDDLE AND LATER LIFE

Mid-life Crisis

Some people may experience a mid-life crisis when they reach middle age and feel dissatisfied with their life. Seek counselling and find ways to channel your energy into positive pursuits. Taking up a new hobby or sport may help. Changing jobs or finally studying what you have always desired may also be healing. It may be time to take that trip you have planned all your life. Be careful not to do anything too drastic as you may regret it later on. Think of how your actions may affect your family, friends, work colleagues. Appreciate what you have and the people around you. Do not take them for granted. It may be time to nourish your spiritual life.

Children leaving home may create a huge void for stay-at-home parents and for those working as well. The home may seem too quiet and lifeless. This is an enormous adjustment for everyone. For parents, it is a time of adjusting to a new relationship with your adult children, adapting to a more peaceful life and greater freedom and time on your hands. Your relationship with your partner may be enriched as you get to know one another again on deeper levels and have more opportunities to explore your interests and spiritual growth. With this change, it may also be a time you can reach out to others in need.

Ageing

In western society there is so much focus on youthful looks, beauty and fashion, it can create fear and dread of ageing, but this is a natural process. The gradual lining of the face and greying of the hair would be better relished as the time approaches of greater freedom and time to pursue interests and spiritual growth.

In relationships, it can be a great time of sharing and peace. It may be the time to finally achieve unfulfilled dreams. It may be the time to celebrate simplicity and rejoice in the beauty of the garden you have created or a painting you have finally painted. It is a time to enjoy your family and friends at a slower pace. It is a gift to be embraced.

Loss of former work or pursuits may lead to grief and loss or depression. Seek counselling and find other ways to channel your energy. Volunteering is an excellent opportunity to help other humans, animals and the environment and add meaning to your twilight years. Playing sport or undertaking creative pursuits may also add joy to your life. There may be opportunities for you to teach young people something you have knowledge of through schools, sporting organisations, youth groups, cubs and scouts. It is important to keep the mind and body active. Don't retire to the couch.

Loss of physical abilities

This is difficult and involves acceptance and letting go. You need to find doable activities and interests to occupy your mind. It is a great opportunity for spiritual growth.

Grief and Loss

With change on any level, there may be grief and loss. When you experience this, tears are healing to allow the grief to flow, as is counselling and possibly joining a support group. If you have lost a family member or friend, sharing memories is helpful, as is exercise and talking to whoever has passed as if they are still with you. Nowness is useful. Take things slowly, and gradually, you will feel acceptance and peace with this change in your life.

Respect

There is lack of respect for the elderly in modern western culture. Not so in Asia or India, where the elderly are revered and cared for within the family. This needs to be turned around. We need to love, care for and respect the elderly—they are a wealth of knowledge and potential teachers—not just the faceless old to be pushed into retirement villages and nursing homes to await their death.

Embrace it

This may be the best period of your life. Enjoy it and make the most of your twilight years.

Spirituality

With more time, your spiritual life may intensify as you pray, read, contemplate, meditate, and maybe, teach others what you have learnt.

Chapter Five
THE WORLD AS IT IS

Masculine energy dominates this world. Too many politicians and business leaders are caught up in ego. There is rampant materialism and greed with too little care for personal wellbeing or that of the environment. The desire for more material possessions such as new model cars and gadgets, new houses and processed food—and population growth—drive onward environmental destruction worldwide which is not without consequence.

Without empathy, there is a lack of understanding others' ethnicity, culture, tribe, religion, sexual preference, socio-economic background or lifestyle choices. Without empathy, there is discrimination, group hatred, conflict, violence and war. War consumes energy, money, life—masculine energy devouring itself. The Earth needs a stop to war.

Feminine energy encompasses gentleness and caring for others and the Earth. It can turn the present situation around through understanding, communication and compassion.

Men need to leave their ego and fighting ways behind. The Earth is at such a cross roads that such needless waste of energy, money and life can only lead to negative consequences.

With a return to feminine energy and caring for the planet there is still some hope for better times before Earth's man-made darkest night envelopes her.

Chapter Six
NATURE

Seeing planet Earth from Space is an amazing and beautiful sight and it seems unbelievable that man has wrought so much destruction upon her.

In nature, where man's footprint has been minimal, there is a feeling of rightness, completeness, harmony and balance. In a green rainforest amongst the tall trees, moss, emerald lichens, ferns, trickling water, birds rustling through the undergrowth—a human may feel the harmony and completeness of life there, how God intended it to be. We want to feel that harmony and completeness within ourselves. The world is broken as nature is broken and so too is humanity.

Time is running out and we need to reduce global warming, stop deforestation and the loss of habitat, overfishing, soil erosion, pollution and other environmental disasters. We need to act now if there is to be any future for the Earth's creatures and humanity.

There needs to be a return to a feminine approach of nurturing. The Earth needs our love and care as much as our children do. We need to try to live harmoniously within nature's balance which will take great effort on the part of governments, miners, manufacturers, forest managers, fishers, farmers and all consumers.

Masculine energy and population growth have created ongoing and growing materialism, greed, wars and environmental destruction. There is no way forward except a return to feminine energy and simplicity to recover what has been lost.

With a return to balance the Earth may recover and become the place of great health and beauty, God's garden, which she was created to be.

Chapter Seven
THE SPIRITUAL LIFE

I See God

I see God in the smiling eyes of a child in the Nepalese mountains
I see God in the complexity of the rainforest in Malaysia
I see God in city streets
I feel Him as I walk
He is there, with us, all, all the time
He just needs to hear your call, to open your eyes to Him
Feel that love
In faith is love and oneness

A life without God may be meaningful to a human being, but a life with God is enriched and directed. Such a human being becomes fulfilled, at peace and cultivates the nourishment of her soul.

The spiritual life encompasses dedication and faith in God. It embodies a loving human who cares for others, animals and nature. He finds his talents and shares them with the world to make it a better place. He does the best he can in whatever circumstances he finds himself in while considering the needs and desires of those around him.

He is aware of himself as a spiritual being, here to learn and help others. He pays attention to details and tries to live a harmonious existence with gratitude.

Contrasts in life are necessary as without seeing the darkness there would be no appreciation of the light. Lifting the darkness from your soul may propel you towards the light within you and surrounding all that is.

To care for the soul requires oneness with God, meditation, prayer, simplicity, appreciation and love of self, others, animals, all of nature and God.

Nowness is living with full awareness in present time with attention to others and the environment around you. Listening attentively is cultivating as is empathy.

Focusing on tasks without distraction in nowness helps you live the spiritual life as does doing things you love, following your chosen life path with passion and taking time to be joy filled and giving by undertaking things such as visiting an elderly relative, making a cake with your children, writing a card to a distant friend, volunteering, greeting a lonely old man.

This is spiritual work as much as meditation and prayer. We are in the human body to experience this physical world and our inter-connectedness enriches our soulful life.

Doing what you love, whether for work or pleasure, connects you to the spiritual as your soul draws sustenance and you are in nowness as you paint, ski, gallop your horse, dance, play with your children, walk, build a house, create a garden or communicate with a customer. There are many ways to nourish your soul, but make it a priority and you will attain greater harmony, peace and wellbeing.

Create moments of peace and stillness—yes stillness. This will nourish your soul. As will a simple life. Complications and too many possessions crowd your time and thoughts. Simplify, and your life will nurture your soul.

A soulful life connects you to God and all that is

Meditation is useful to attain stillness and oneness with God—to be free of the babble of the mind and rest in that infinite stillness.

Meditation may be achieved through peaceful relaxation in nature, gentle exercise, nowness, classes, courses or listening to guided meditation.

Your whole life can be a meditative experience as you keep in mind that you are a spiritual being here to learn and give with awareness of your thoughts and feelings and your impact upon other human beings, animals, plants and the Earth. Conscious moment-to-moment living with awareness is soulful.

Prayer connects you to God through speaking to Him as your ally in life. Thankfulness, forgiveness, caring for others, the world in general, other countries, nature, assistance—all these things and more can be part of your prayer talk. Don't be afraid. Speak to Him as your dearest friend. He is there for you, always.

Prayer enriches the spiritual life.

Spiritual growth is like the growth of a plant, requiring nurturing, and slowly, little by little, it reaches upwards towards the light. Sometimes it may need pruning as it heads in the wrong direction, sometimes growth may stall, but eventually it reaches its magnificence, becoming what it was meant to be, a glowing light upon this Earth, illuminating all that it comes into contact with, walking beside God, in godliness.

God is there

Upon the dew on the spider's web on a winter morning
In the gurgling water falling over boulders
In a stranger's smile
With the Autumn falling leaves and the winter crackling fire
As the sun sets and twilight glows
God is there, an all loving, all-encompassing God

Death is not to be feared. It is a doorway to a new beginning and onward growth of the soul.

Contemplation of death leads to an appreciation of life. If you know death is near, or contemplate its approach, the layers of your life may peel away down to the bare essentials of what makes you happy, what is important and what gives you peace.

Life involves the gradual letting go—letting go of youth, material possessions, old ideas, outworn relationships, physical and mental capacities, outgrown lifestyles, loved ones. Letting go can be difficult and emotional but at the same time liberating as life becomes simpler, allowing greater time for soulful pursuits.

The ultimate release is the release of the body at death. Do not be afraid.

Chapter Eight
LOOKING FORWARD

As we look at the world as it is, the outlook may seem dismal with so many wars; discrimination; persecution; inequality; environmental destruction; species extinction and being threatened with extinction; pollution; global warming; rampant materialism; alienating urban life for many; social problems abounding.

There is hope if we can all become more soulful, tune into our spirituality and feel empathy for all of humanity, animals and nature. With that so many problems would diminish.

A feminine energy needs to embrace planet Earth so that no longer, the aggressive, dominating and materialistic male energy wreaks havoc. With the feminine energy will come a caring attitude to all of life and a harmonious existence may ensue—but time is of the essence—the time is now.

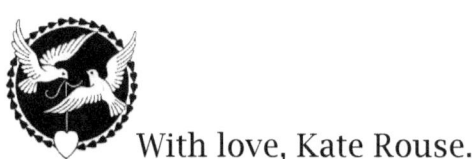 With love, Kate Rouse.

www.ingramcontent.com/pod-product-compliance
Lightning Source LLC
Chambersburg PA
CBHW072057290426
44110CB00014B/1724